ROSIE
Backstage

WRITTEN BY

Amanda Lewis AND Tim Wynne-Jones

ILLUSTRATED BY

Bill Slavin

Kids Can Press Ltd.
Toronto

Kids Can Press Ltd. acknowledges with appreciation the assistance of the Canada Council and the Ontario Arts Council in the production of this book.

Canadian Cataloguing in Publication Data

Lewis, Amanda
    Rosie backstage

ISBN 1-55074-209-4 (bound)   ISBN 1-55074-148-9 (pbk.)

1. Repertory theater - Juvenile literature.   2. Theater - Juvenile literature.   3. Theater - Production and direction - Juvenile literature.   I. Wynne-Jones, Tim.   II. Slavin, Bill. III. Title.

PN2037.L48 1994   j792   C94-930168-X

Kids Can Press Ltd.
29 Birch Avenue
Toronto, Ontario, Canada
M4V 1E2

Edited by Charis Wahl
Interior designed by Michael Solomon and Esperança Melo
Cover designed by Esperança Melo
Printed and bound in Hong Kong

94 0 9 8 7 6 5 4 3 2 1

ACKNOWLEDGEMENTS

The authors would like to gratefully acknowledge the assistance of David William, Elliott Hayes and Pat Quigley of the Stratford Festival Theatre (Ontario). We'd also like to thank the many helpful and imaginative people who work backstage at the Festival and who generously gave us their time, expertise and anecdotes, allowing us a glimpse into their busy world. As well, special thanks go to David Jacklin for advice on stage fighting; Dr. John MacPherson, K.M., for clarification of details on the Globe Theatre; Delvalle Dasilva Lewis for her squawking chicken; and Ellen Stafford for her constant support and love of theatre. Bob Newland of Fanfare Books has been both generous and enthusiastic. And the Ontario Arts Council, through a writers reserve grant, certainly helped get things started. Our deep gratitude goes to our editor, Charis Wahl, whose unflagging sense of humour lit up our dark stages; Bill Slavin, whose illustrations have been an inspiration from the start; and Valerie Hussey, for suggesting we do this together and who, along with the perceptive staff at Kids Can Press, made it possible not only to survive the process but to have a good time! And finally, we'd like to thank Xan, Maddy and Lewis, who see the magic.

To Tom, Diana and Eleanor, our favourite theatrical family — AL & TWJ

To Alan and Linda, with love — BS

CHAPTER 1

R OSIE sat cross-legged on the floor of Caliban's
cave. The monster crouched opposite her,
tugging at his face. Footsteps squeaked overhead,
and the voice of Prospero, the magician, boomed:

*"Thou poisonous slave, got by the devil himself
Upon thy wicked dam, come forth!"*

"That's your cue," Rosie whispered. Caliban
frantically jumped to his feet and pushed on the trapdoor above their heads. It wouldn't budge. He cursed
a monster curse. Rosie tried to help but the door was
stuck.

"Take this," whispered Caliban, ripping off his
mask. "I can't see a thing."

The floor of the stage above them creaked with approaching steps. Then something rapped on the trapdoor.

"Yoohoo, Caliban. Nice doggy!"

Rosie looked anxiously at Caliban. It was not Prospero's voice, and those were not words from the play.

One, two, three — heave! The door gave at last, and Rosie and the maskless wild man spilled onto the stage. The director's shiny black toe tapped inches from Rosie's nose. Somebody giggled, but not the director. He glared.

"How nice of you to show up," he snapped at Caliban. Beside him stood Prospero.

7

"Caliban's underling, I presume," the actor said in a deep, gentle voice.

"At your service," said Rosie, holding up the monster's mask to her face.

Prospero smiled. But not the director.

"What is this, social hour? We're trying to rehearse a play!" He strode off the stage and into the seats of the theatre where there was a table littered with notes, thick file folders and coffee cups.

"Sorry," said Rosie, but the director just sighed and barked at the stage manager beside him. "Margaret, have the mechanism on that trapdoor checked."

She nodded. "I've made a note of it." She looked at her watch. It was time for everyone to take their morning break.

"Break," Margaret called loudly so all the actors and stagehands could hear. "We'll resume act one, scene two in twenty minutes."

"Fifteen," growled the director, stomping down the tunnel exit under the seats.

Rosie breathed a sigh of relief when he had gone. It was a noisy sigh. Several people laughed out loud. One laugh came from a shadowy figure sitting halfway up the aisle. No one but Rosie noticed him.

"Our esteemed director is having a bad morning," said Prospero beside her. He looked old and weary, but his voice was warm.

Caliban hoisted himself out of the trap opening. In the light he wasn't much of a monster, just Rosie's friend Angelo.

"Thanks for your help, Rosie," Angelo said gloomily, as he walked across the stage to talk to Margaret. "It pinches my nose," he explained, handing her the mask.

"Rosie," Margaret called. "Could

you take this mask back to the props department?"
She smiled. "We can use all the help we can get."

"Sure," said Rosie, glad to have something to do. As
she took the mask, she noticed something move in
the seats. The man who had laughed at her noisy sigh
stood up, walked into the deeper shadows and
seemed to disappear.

Rosie followed the pathway below the stage
towards the props room. She hurried, afraid she might
run into the director. "What a grouch," she said,
grimacing at the warty mask of Caliban.

❖ ❖ ❖

Rosie and her mother, Cleo, had been in Stratford
only a week. Cleo was replacing the props mistress,
who had suddenly fallen sick. Rosie's father was on
tour with his band in Australia, so Rosie found herself
hanging around the huge theatre. She didn't know
anyone except Angelo: his daughter, Zoë, was Rosie's
best friend back home. But Zoë wasn't coming to
Stratford until school was finished, and Angelo and
Rosie's mom had to work all day, so there was no one
for Rosie to play with.

She had thought it would be fun to be out of
school a month early, but now she wasn't so sure.

On her way to the props room, Rosie cautiously
peered into a rehearsal hall where she had first seen
The Grouch at work. He had been moving people
around on a rehearsal stage exactly like the real stage
in the theatre. Today only two of the actors, Alice and
Stephen, were in the room — lying on the floor, their
hands resting on their stomachs. They
were making weird noises.

"Mmmmmaaahhh."

"Are you all right?" Rosie asked.

"Just doing our warm-ups," said
Alice. Rosie edged into the room.

"Huh! Huh! Huh!" barked Stephen.
"Just sharpening our rusty tools."

These two are crazy, thought Rosie.

"An actor's body and voice are tools,"
said Alice, "and just like a hammer
or a saw, they can get dull and rusty.
We have to exercise to keep them
in shape."

"I know how to exercise my body,"
Rosie said, "but how do you exercise
your voice?"

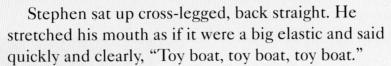

Stephen sat up cross-legged, back straight. He stretched his mouth as if it were a big elastic and said quickly and clearly, "Toy boat, toy boat, toy boat."

Alice added, "Unique New York, unique New York, unique New York." She looked at Rosie. "Try it."

Rosie cleared her throat. "Unique New York. Unik u nuck, ununk noo what?" Her tongue felt as if it were glued to the roof of her mouth.

"Your tongue and face muscles could use some exercise, Rosie," said Alice, laughing.

Pulling her down to sit beside them, Stephen said, "We also do breathing and singing exercises. Try saying 'Huh! Huh! Huh!' the way I did."

Rosie tried, but only a small sound came out.

"It's too much in your chest," said Alice. She placed her hand on the small of Rosie's back. "Make the sound come from way down."

Taking a deep breath, Rosie barked out a deep "Huh" that made the room shake. Alice and Stephen clapped. Rosie beamed.

"Your voice has to be loud enough to carry to all the seats in the theatre," explained Alice. "But you can't just yell every show, night after night. That would hurt your voice."

"And yelling sounds pretty stupid in a love scene," said Stephen.

"But how does your voice get loud without yelling?" asked Rosie.

"By letting the sound come from your whole body, not just your vocal cords. That's called resonance." Stephen took Alice's hands.

"*O Rosalind, these trees shall be my books,*
And in their barks my thoughts I'll character,
That every eye which in this forest looks
Shall see thy virtue witness'd every where."

Although Stephen only whispered, Rosie could hear the words all around her.

Rosie tried to whisper resonantly, but what came out was a low croak. "I guess my tools are a little rusty."

"It takes time," said Alice, "but at your stage that wasn't bad."

Stage! Rosie leaped to her feet, a vision of The Grouch filling her head. "Gotta run," she said. Scooping up Caliban's mask, she scooted down the hall to the props room.

Actors' Tongue-twisters

Try saying some of these tongue-twisters to exercise your mouth muscles. Say each one quickly and clearly three times.

Round and round the rough and rugged rock the ragged rascal ran.

A noise annoys an oyster but a noisy noise annoys an oyster more.

Old oily Ollie oils old oily autos.

Betty bought some butter. "But," she said, "this butter's bitter, and a bit of better butter would make a better batter." So she bought a bit of butter better than the bitter butter and she put it in her batter and her batter was not bitter.

CHAPTER 2

*B*UT I glued them on perfectly," said Jamie unhappily.

Cleo was scowling at a huge green cloak with white splotches around the neck. "Somebody must have ripped them off!"

"Ripped what off?" asked Rosie, coming through the door of the props room.

"Jamie had glued a pattern of diamonds around the border of the cloak and they've vanished," Cleo said.

"A diamond thief?" asked Rosie.

"Hardly, honey." Cleo sounded tired. "And where have you been? Angelo was by on his break, so I know all about this mask." Rosie started to explain about Alice and Stephen, but her mother wasn't listening.

"The nostrils shouldn't be hard to alter, but they'll have to wait. Right now we've got to get the new jewels formed up for the Duke's cloak. Oh, and Jamie, the director wants to see oval ornaments this time, not diamond-shaped ones."

"Humph!" Jamie switched on the Vacuform machine to warm up. "I wish he'd make up his mind."

Rosie hopped up on the counter. "Did the director steal the diamonds?"

Jamie made a face. "We're jinxed," he whispered.

Cleo was exasperated. "Rosie, please. Jamie's got a lot of work to do."

Rosie sighed. It was a morning for grumps and grouches. She watched Jamie put some oval shapes made of modelling clay on a special tray. The tray went into the Vacuform machine along with a thick sheet of clear plastic.

Every shelf in the props room was piled high with
bits of fur and reels of wire and cans of paint. There
was fruit to paint, a velvet purse to embroider, the
skeleton of an umbrella, a half-finished sword. Cleo
and Jamie were working on props for two plays: *The
Tempest*, the one with Caliban and Prospero, and
Macbeth. Everything for *As You Like It* — including
the green cloak — was supposed to have been
finished weeks ago.

Jamie pressed a button on the Vacuform machine,
and the plastic sheet dropped over the forms.
Intense heat melted the plastic into the shape of the
oval moulds. It made Rosie think of grocery-store
chicken in cellophane, except that this wrap cooled
hard and solid.

When the plastic had cooled down, Jamie took it out of the machine and cut out each oval shape.

"Can I help paint?" Rosie asked.

"Sure," said Jamie.

"No," said Cleo. "Honey, I'm sorry. There just isn't time to teach you right now."

Rosie gave Cleo her most sullen look. Her mother glared back and shoved a painted apple into the mouth of a pretend roast pig.

The pig did not look pleased.

Props

The props department has to find or make all the things that the actors need on stage. Props must be easy to use, lightweight and durable. The Vacuform machine can make all sorts of detailed shapes, from jewellery to a roast pig. If a play needs soldiers outfitted in armour, the props people make a breastplate mould of modelling clay. It can be used in the Vacuform machine to create as many plastic copies as are required. When the plastic has cooled, it can be painted to look like solid steel or decorated with fake gems. The plastic is hard and strong, and makes a satisfying *thunk* when hit with a prop sword.

Imagine a merchant in an old-fashioned market. He appears to be carrying a live chicken in a crate. During every performance, right on cue, the chicken has to squawk and crash around inside the crate. How would you make such a prop?

Cleo wound up a wooden stick with elastic bands (like a propeller), put it in a crate filled with feathers and held it in place with a latch. When the actor released the latch, the stick twirled and clattered against the crate and feathers flew out between the slats. Instant chicken!

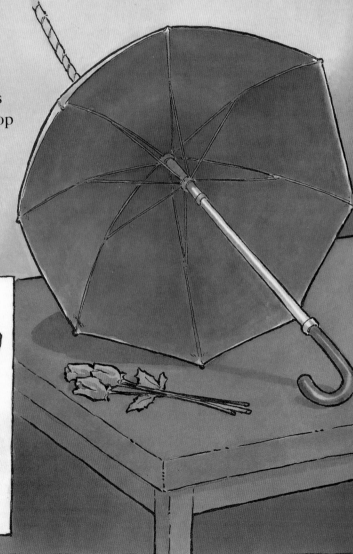

Props — even fake chickens — are set out on a table backstage before each show, and must be returned so they can be found when needed.

Sometimes a prop will have to change in appearance during the play. An umbrella that looks fine in act 1 may have to looked ripped apart in act 4. A purse may have to be covered in mud in one scene and clean by the next. The props people will get two identical umbrellas and rip one up. They'll get two identical purses and slap mud all over one. Both umbrellas and both purses will sit on the props table so the actors can take the right one on stage for each scene.

The people in props need to know how to sew, glue, paint, carve, mould and how to be very inventive!

Des, from the costume department, appeared at the door.

"May I borrow Rosie?" he asked. "Just for a couple of minutes?"

"Be my guest," said Cleo.

Rosie frowned.

"I'm making a tunic for Macduff's son, and I want to see how it looks," said Des.

"You want me to be a boy?"

"The kid playing the part isn't feeling well," said Des. "You're about his size."

"Well, at least *someone* thinks I'm useful," said Rosie, just loud enough for her mom to hear.

In the costume department, things were humming. Des led Rosie over to his work space. "I'd like you to meet Judy," he said, introducing her to a clothes dummy covered with bits of cream-coloured cloth.

"Hi, Judy," said Rosie. "Boring job you've got." Then Des took the bits of cloth off Judy and pinned them over Rosie's T-shirt.

"This is dumb," Rosie blurted out. "Not only is the job boring, but this cloth is boring."

"This is just the cotton muslin we use as a pattern." Des showed her a sketch of a boy in a costume. Attached to it were little pieces of colourful material from which the real costume would be made.

"Now hold still," said Des.

"He looks scared," said Rosie.

"So would you if you were about to be murdered!"

"Ouch!" said Rosie.

Des had accidentally pricked her with a pin. Holding still was not one of Rosie's strong points.

Costume Designer

The costume designer works with the director to create a special look for each character. Each costume reveals facts about the character's social position, personality, tastes and habits. But whether a character is rich or poor, showy or sloppy, all the costumes for all the characters must go together. In this way, the costume designer creates a look for the whole play.

The costume designer makes a sketch of each actor as his or her character. These sketches are based on information in the play and on the director's ideas about that character. The designer creates a sketch for each change of clothing the character needs and chooses the fabrics to use.

The actor's measurements, a description of every costume and swatches of the fabrics are given to the cutters and sewers in the costume department, and they transform the sketch into reality.

ACT IV SCENE ii
~MACDUFF'S SON~

Costumes

The costume department at a large theatre may have up to 150 people making a thousand costumes every year. They sort material, iron, cut and sew. Some costumes are remodelled: dyed a different colour or taken apart, recut and made into something else. But many have to be made entirely from scratch.

Costumes have to *look* very real, but looks can sometimes be deceiving. A suit of chain-mail armour can be knitted from lightweight cotton yarn and sprayed with metallic paint. Even up close it will look as though it was fashioned from strong metal chains. But for some costumes there are no short cuts. An elaborate wedding dress might take 250 hours to make — and cost thousands of dollars.

Jewellery

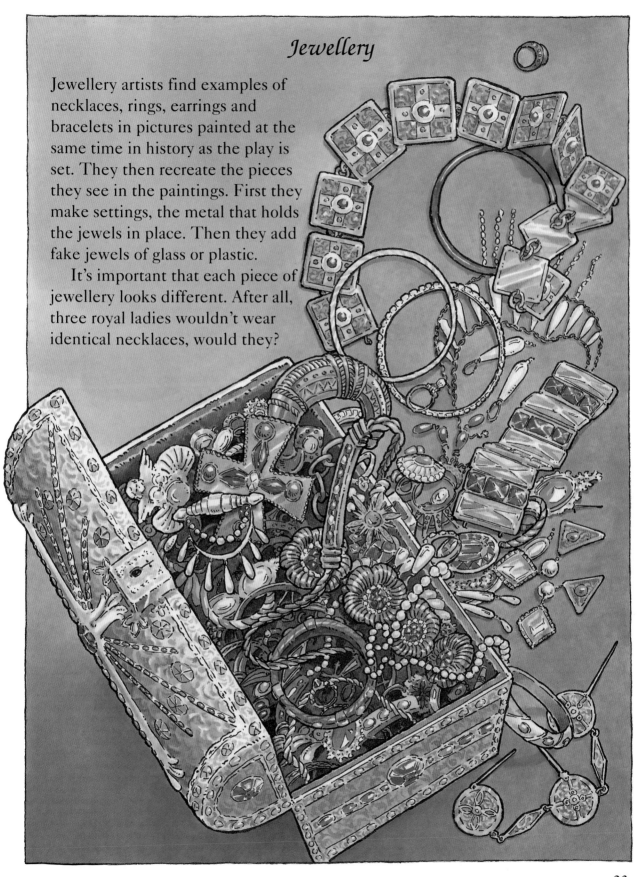

Jewellery artists find examples of necklaces, rings, earrings and bracelets in pictures painted at the same time in history as the play is set. They then recreate the pieces they see in the paintings. First they make settings, the metal that holds the jewels in place. Then they add fake jewels of glass or plastic.

It's important that each piece of jewellery looks different. After all, three royal ladies wouldn't wear identical necklaces, would they?

Milliner

Once the best hat makers in Europe were to be found in the city of Milan, in Italy. So a hat maker was called a "Milaner." Today's milliner at a large theatre has to be able to recreate hats from many different countries and times.

A hat is formed on a wooden head-like shape called a block. The hat department has more than one hundred blocks in various sizes to match actors' head sizes. There are also different blocks for different styles of hat.

Stiff cloth, called buckram, or soft felt shapes are used to make the basic hat. Buckram is cut into whatever shape is needed. "Unblocked" felt, that is, felt that has not been shaped yet, comes pre-made in soft floppy shapes in a variety of colours. To form the hat, the buckram or felt shapes are steamed or soaked, then stretched onto the block to dry overnight.

After the felt is dry, it is lacquered to make it hard. Buckram does not need to be hardened. Instead, it is covered in whatever fabric the designer chooses. Wire is put along the brim of the hat to make it hold its shape. The hat can then be trimmed with feathers, flowers, ribbons — whatever is needed to give the right effect.

Top hats, straw hats with flowers, tiny caps made of lace, soft purple hats with plumes — more than 250 different hats are created each season. The milliner for a theatre has to have quite a head for fashion!

Cobbler

Because plays take place at any time and place in history, the actors can't just wear their runners! A full-time cobbler, or shoemaker, is needed to keep the actors comfortably on their toes.

Shoes and boots have to look right and be comfortable, but they must also be flexible and safe. Actors run, jump, dance and fight on stage. Badly made shoes can cause an accident so great care must be taken. Special rubber or non-skid soles are used to keep the actors from slipping.

Shoes are usually made of leather or felt and dyed or spray-painted the right colour. Every year the Stratford cobblers make about 150 pairs of shoes. Hundreds of other pairs are bought and customized to suit the characters on stage.

CHAPTER 3

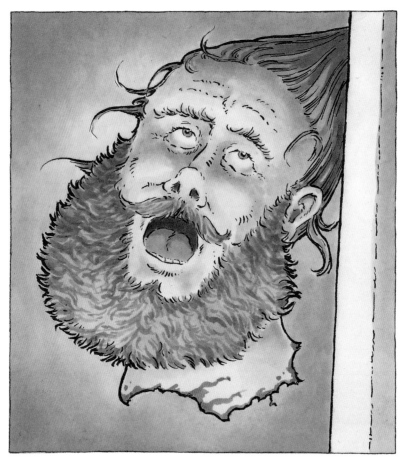

Rosie screamed! Dangling right in front of her face, framed by the props-room door, was a severed head, its neck all drippy with blood. The head bobbed up and down. Then Jamie poked his head around the corner, laughing.

"Gotcha!" he said. "The director called — wants to have a look at this. Guess who gets to deliver it?"

Rosie took hold of the hank of black hair squeamishly. "It's disgusting. Who is this guy, anyway?"

Jamie cocked an eyebrow. "Let's just say it's for 'the Scottish play.'"

"The Scottish play? You mean *Macbeth*?"

The room grew suddenly quiet. Jamie's face went

white. Everyone was staring at Rosie.

"Uh-oh. Now you've done it," said Cleo.

"Done what?" asked Rosie. "All I said was —"

"Shhh," said Cleo, clapping a hand over Rosie's mouth.

"It's very bad luck to say the name of the Scottish play in a theatre," said Jamie solemnly. "You'll have to leave the room, turn around three times, spit and ask politely to be let back in."

"You've got to be kidding," said Rosie. But every face told her that they were all perfectly serious.

"This is silly," she said as everyone watched her turning and spitting. "Please may I come back in now?" she asked with forced politeness, expecting them to laugh as she re-entered the room.

They didn't.

"You may think it's silly," said Jamie, "but we've got troubles enough without any more bad luck."

Cleo pointed to the door. "The director won't wait all day for that head," she said. "Off you go."

Annoyed, Rosie stamped out of the room, bloody head in hand, to face The Grouch. What a day!

Superstitions

When you make a mistake on stage, hundreds, sometimes thousands, of people see it. Perhaps this is why theatre people tend to be superstitious. It is considered *bad* luck to wish anyone *good* luck — an invitation for mischievous forces to do their worst. That's why people say "Break a leg" to an actor before a performance. Wishing for bad luck is supposed to bring good luck. In German opera and theatre, they go one step further. Their wish, *Hals und Beinbruch*, means break your neck and legs!

Some theatre people believe that tripping as you walk on stage is lucky, because it gets the bad luck over with. Others say that tripping means you'll forget your lines.

Whistling backstage is thought to cause a bad performance. It might "bring down the house" — that is, the audience may whistle and boo so loud that the play will have to stop. (Whistling in mines is bad luck, too. Miners don't want to "bring down the house," either!)

Quoting from *Macbeth* — or even saying the name of the play — is absolutely the worst bad luck. Accidents, even deaths, have happened during productions of *Macbeth*. One young actor apparently began quoting *Macbeth* backstage, laughing at a fellow actor's superstitious fears. Moments later the actors on stage began to get hurt — broken toes, broken fingers and bruised shins. As for the young actor,

he was hit by a car when he left the theatre that day!

In 1703, during a production of *Macbeth*, England was hit by the worst storm in its history. Fifteen hundred sailors were drowned, millions of dollars' damage was done in London and the city of Bristol was flattened. Some people thought the hurricane was God's wrath against a play that had witches and black magic in it. London theatres were closed for a week.

Some say *Macbeth* is bad luck because Shakespeare used real witches' spells in the play and they attract real evil spirits. Just in case, actors are careful never to make fun of spirits and always refer to *Macbeth* as the Scottish play.

❖ ❖ ❖

Rosie made her way very slowly to the stage. Carrying the head of a dead king whose name you couldn't say was almost as bad as having to face The Grouch again.

Past the work rooms and the rehearsal studio there were no windows and the light was dim.

"You think you've got it bad," she said glumly to the severed head. "I wish I'd never come here."

Suddenly a voice startled her.

"*Thou liest, thou shag-ear'd villain.*"

Rosie froze and almost dropped the head. Someone stepped out from a corner of the hall. It was the man who had laughed at her noisy sigh in the theatre.

He approached her, smiling. His hair hung shoulder length. He had a small pointy beard and one gold earring. He turned the severed head so that he could see its face. "*Behold where stands th' usurper's cursed head.* It's very good."

"I think it looks pretty phoney," Rosie said, recovering her bravery.

"Ah, but you haven't seen the magic yet. Under the right lights it will look marvellous."

"The director wants to see it right now," Rosie said importantly, continuing down the hall. The man fell in step beside her; his soft pointy slippers made no sound on the concrete floor.

"We didn't have such fancy props in my day."

Aha! So he was an actor, Rosie thought. "What's your name?" she asked.

"Will will do."

"Okay," said Rosie. "So what is it that Will will do?"

"What cheek!" said Will, but he seemed pleased.

"I am a poet, a bard. Indeed, I am sometimes called the Bard of Stratford-Upon-Avon."

"The what?"

"Will Shakespeare, at your service," the man said, bowing deeply.

Rosie laughed. "Yeah, right. Well, I'm Rosie."

"Ah," said Will, "and what is your name in full bloom?"

It took her a moment to figure out what he meant. "Rosalind," she said. "I was named after a character in a play."

"*As You Like It*," said Will.

"How did you know?"

"We bards know all sorts of things." As they reached the back entrance to the stage, Will said, "This is where I must leave you."

"Do you have to? Couldn't you come along and help me deliver this thing?" Rosie tried not to sound nervous.

"I'm afraid not," he said. "But we'll meet again." Then he bowed low, turned on his heel and was gone, humming a jaunty tune.

Rosie looked at the severed head. "Ready?" She made the head nod. "Prepare to meet thy doom," she said, and stepped through the curtains.

CHAPTER 4

*T*HE stage was in chaos. There was noise and movement in every corner. Men up high on scaffolding were attaching thick rope riggings to hooks in the ceiling. Several large rock-like shapes were being moved around the stage. A ship's cabin was being fitted over the trapdoor that had been Caliban's cave.

The crew was making a shipwreck for the opening scene of *The Tempest*. Through the disorder and jumble Rosie could see the director poring over diagrams and sketches with a woman she had not seen earlier. The woman looked up and called to one of the set builders who seemed to be in charge.

"Richard," she said in a thick accent.

Richard came over. They looked at the plans, then he walked over to the man working on the cabin.

"Sorry, Fred, but madame says it should be half a metre higher."

Fred groaned.

"She's the designer, Fred. And she's right. Next time, double-check the plans."

Fred's shoulders drooped. He noticed Rosie standing nearby. Then, seeing the head dangling from her hand, his eyes bulged and he got right back to work.

Set Designer

The set designer must work closely with the director to establish the period and style of the play. This might involve research into how a particular group of people lived in a certain time and place. *The Tempest* starts with a scene of a ship in a storm. But what kind of a ship: an ancient galleon, a royal yacht, a cruise ship? The set is often the first thing that the audience sees. It lets the audience know where and when in history the play takes place. It tells part of the story.

The set can be elaborate and detailed or it can merely suggest a location: one or two trees can stand for a whole forest; a bed and lamp can be a bedroom; a bale of hay and a pitchfork, a barn; a large box and two flashlights, a car. A set can be realistic or fanciful: imagine a dining room where the table, chairs, carpet and sideboard are all striped like a zebra!

Because a set often has to be changed from scene to scene, sets must look solid but actually be light and easy to move. Often large structures — walls, rocks, archways — have to be moved in less than a minute. A huge sailing vessel may have to be replaced by a courtyard as the audience waits and watches. Sets must be designed to be put together and taken apart with ease and efficiency.

The set designer must have the skills of an architect, an interior designer, a historian, a sculptor and a painter. She or he must also know everything that happens in the play. For example, if an actor is to climb up to a balcony, sturdy footholds must be built into the set. And if a character is to look out a window, there must *be* a window to look out or someone is going to feel very foolish!

Setting

A play can be set in any time period the director and designers wish. Shakespeare wrote his plays four hundred years ago. Sometimes they are set to look as they might have looked in Shakespeare's day and sometimes they are set in an earlier time, such as classical Rome or a medieval castle. They can also be set in a time closer to our own. A director might decide to do Shakespeare Western-style, complete with cowboy hats and spurs, or with everyone dressed as 1920s gangsters, machine guns and all! The setting might be elegant or funny, gross or simple. Whatever the director and designers decide, the setting affects the way that the audience *sees* the play and how they interpret or understand it.

Set Builders

Like the people in the props department, the set builders have to be magicians. They must make fake look real: what is light must look heavy, what is hollow must look solid. They must transform a bare stage into a castle, a garden, a living room, a dungeon.

If a set has to have walls, builders usually use "flats." A flat is a wooden frame, normally four feet by eight feet over which a piece of canvas is stretched, tacked and glued. The canvas can then be painted in any style and repainted and reused as often as necessary. Flats can be made with window and door openings and can be hinged together to make whole rooms.

Sometimes set builders need to make large, oddly shaped structures. Moulded wire, Styrofoam and fibreglass are often used because they are lightweight. Wire can be bent into shapes and covered with cloth to become a tree or a boulder; because the object is hollow inside, it is easy to move. Styrofoam, backed with sturdy plywood, can be carved and painted to look like a detailed stone archway. Huge fibreglass rocks can be light enough for one person to carry, but strong enough for a shipload of pirates to dance on.

The magic really begins to happen when the structures are painted. The hull of a ship made of Styrofoam and fibreglass can be painted to look exactly like a huge, barnacle-covered sailing vessel of long ago.

For a set builder, there is no such word as impossible.

The scene was so confusing and noisy that it didn't seem like a good time to be interrupting the director. Rosie just wanted to get out of there. Hurrying to escape unnoticed, she ran smack into a worker carrying a ship's steering wheel.

Crunch.

Rosie's elbow knocked off one of the steering wheel's handles.

"Oh no!" Rosie was almost in tears.

"Hey, it's okay," said the builder. "It'll glue back easily."

But other damage had been done.

"Our Little Mouse again?" The director's voice carried above the clatter of the work crew. "Seems we can't keep you off the stage."

"I was bringing you this," Rosie said, holding the severed head. The director cocked an eyebrow. "What on earth for?"

"You called the props department!" she shouted over the noise. "You asked especially to see, uh, what's-his-name."

"I certainly did *not*. Take that accursed thing away right now," said the director. "I'm in mid-shipwreck, in case you hadn't noticed."

Rosie braced for a long-winded attack — he was building up quite a head of steam — but suddenly everything went dark. A dazzling, hot spotlight hit the stage directly where Rosie stood. The bright light blinded her, and she held up the dead head to protect her eyes. Then someone at the back of the theatre shouted, "Bravo!" and started to clap.

The head was transformed: the eyes glared terrifyingly in their shadowy sockets. Rosie panicked. She hurled the head as far away as she could. It arced through the hot beam of the spotlight and landed in the dark with a thump.

The spotlight died and the regular lights came back on. Everyone stared up at the lighting booth at the back of the theatre. It looked dark and empty.

The director scowled at Rosie. He crossed the cluttered stage and picked up the severed head from a snake-like coil of electrical wire. He held it gingerly at arm's length as he approached her.

"Let the make-up people put on the extra bruises next time," he said, handing the head back to her. "And in future, Little Mouse, *I* will decide when I want to preview the props."

Rosie opened her mouth but was too confused to speak. She just nodded stupidly and hurried off the stage. Once in the wings, she let out her anger in a long, low whistle.

"For goodness' sakes, don't whistle!" Margaret, the stage manager, snapped.

"Oh no, more bad luck?" asked Rosie.

Margaret nodded. "We seem to be having quite a run of it."

Rosie tried to explain that there had been a phone call to bring the head up for inspection. Margaret seemed surprised. "It wasn't me," she said.

Rosie went cold all over.

"Wasn't my assistant, either," said Margaret. "We've been searching everywhere for my prompt book for the Scottish play. It's lost, and if I don't find it, *my* head will look like that one you're carrying! You haven't seen it, have you?"

"Me?"

"I'm beginning to think we really are jinxed this season."

And I'm the jinx! thought Rosie. Oh, why couldn't I have gone with my dad to Australia?

40

Stage Manager

The stage manager is the person who has to know what everyone else is doing. She or he has to be able to answer everyone's questions and solve everyone's problems. A lot of people work together to put on a show — in costumes, lighting, sound, props, sets, make-up, front of house — and the stage manager must make sure that all of them know what they're supposed to be doing.

The stage manager also organizes rehearsals so that all the actors are there when they are needed. During rehearsals, the stage manager must make notes of all the director's decisions — the blocking (where the actors move and when); when lights come on; when a sound cue happens; changes in costumes, props or sets ("That wall should be blue, not green"); everything that needs fixing or that hasn't been done yet.

A prompt book contains all the information about the actual running of the play. It might be a three-ring binder or scrapbook. On one page is a page from the play. Across from it might be an outline of the stage, on which the stage manager draws little arrows to show where the actor is to move. Beside each arrow a number indicates when in the play the actor is supposed to go there. If an actor forgets his or her moves or lines, the stage manager can find them in the book. Other numbers are used to remind the stage manager of the sound and light cues. During the actual run of the show, the stage manager can make sure that the sounds and lights happen when they are supposed to.

You can read a stage manager's prompt book and, with a little imagination, see and hear the whole play in your mind's eye.

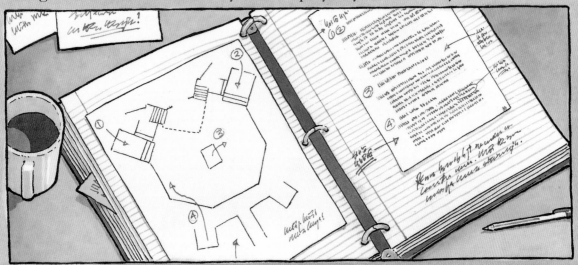

CHAPTER 5

*F*IRST Caliban and now that Scottish king whose name you can't say. I'm spending all my time lugging around somebody's ugly face," Rosie muttered to herself as she headed back to the props department. Why did she feel so miserable? It wasn't her fault that everything was going wrong.

She kept thinking about the spotlight. Who could have pulled that prank? Why on her? She decided to check out the lighting booth. Nobody was in a hurry for the severed head. And, she thought, nobody wants me around, either.

The lighting booth was two floors up at the back of the theatre. She arrived a little breathless to find Toby, the lighting technician, at the computer.

"So it was you!" Rosie sputtered. "What kind of a practical joke was that? Are you trying to get me murdered?"

Toby looked up, puzzled. "Hi. You're Cleo's kid, aren't you?"

Rosie humphed. "Here I am trying not to be noticed and suddenly — zap! — you hit me with that spotlight!"

"Whoa, calm down. What spotlight? What are you talking about? I just got in."

"Well, *someone* was here," said Rosie.

Toby looked dubious. "I don't see how. This door is always kept locked — there's a lot of valuable equipment in here." Toby gestured towards the control panel. With all its buttons and lights it looked like something out of *Star Trek*.

"But you know I had a funny feeling when I first unlocked the booth," said Toby. "I could have sworn that there was someone in the room." She smiled at Rosie. "But that's just not possible."

Rosie looked around with a little shiver and hugged the severed head.

Toby laughed. "That's a pretty weird security blanket."

Lighting, like sets and costumes, is specifically designed for each show. But good lighting seems invisible — it's only when something goes wrong that the audience notices. Imagine an actor in the centre of the stage speaking in total darkness while across from him, the stairs are brightly lit! Proper light helps the audience to focus on what is important to see. It also helps to create the mood of a scene.

Lights of many sizes and shapes are used to create different effects on stage. They are all carefully hung on metal bars high above the stage and aimed at specific places on the stage. "Gels," thin pieces of coloured plastic, are put in front of the bulbs to change the colour of the light. A scene bathed in pale blue light will seem cold and forbidding. The same scene bathed in orange will look warm and inviting.

The lighting designer and the director decide when certain lights should come on and how bright each should be. The lighting technician then programs these lighting cues into a computerized lighting system so that the lights will come on at their proper level at the push of a button.

The technician can see the stage from the lighting booth and can talk through an intercom with the stage manager, who says when to begin a lighting cue and thus change the lighting on the stage.

In Shakespeare's day, plays were performed outside, in the afternoon by sunlight.

A hundred years ago, the stage was lit by gaslights. These footlights sat on the floor along the front of the stage. They made it possible for plays to be performed indoors, but because they shone from below, they made the actors' faces look strange and rather scary. With the invention of electricity, lights could shine down on actors' faces much more naturally, like real sunlight or moonlight.

Today, electric lights and computerized lighting systems have allowed for the creation of extra-ordinary special effects. And, of course, shows can be performed indoors at any hour of any season.

Toby gave Rosie a smile. "Look, to pull that trick a person would have to know this panel really well. First of all, you'd have to know which switches control the work lights. Those are the ones that are on now. You'd have to kill those — turn them off — to get a blackout. Then you'd have to call up the one light aimed at where you were standing. No one knows that cue except me. And I have the only key to the booth." Toby shrugged. "So I don't see how it could have happened."

"It happened, all right," said Rosie. "Just ask The Grouch — I mean, the director!"

Toby grinned as she turned back to her work.

Rosie left the booth, talking to the bloody head in her hands. "There's something fishy going on around here, and I'm going to get to the bottom of it!"

The next day Rosie decided to stay out of everyone's way. She hid high up in the sound booth overlooking the stage — "the best seat in the house," Owen called it.

Owen was the sound engineer. He was playing different recordings of thunder for the director, who was down on the floor of the stage. Rosie sat on a low stool in the corner of the little room where The Grouch couldn't see her.

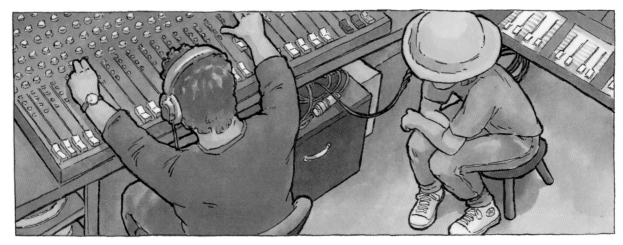

46

Sound

In Shakespeare's theatre, there was a special platform for the musicians and sound-effects people. Rain, for instance, was created by bouncing dried peas on an upside-down drum skin; thunder was made by rolling cannon balls along boards.

Today, theatres use both live and recorded sounds. Recordings can be played through speakers throughout the theatre so that the sound comes from all around, or, played from one speaker to another, the sound can seem to be travelling.

Recordings of some sounds can be borrowed from sound libraries, then changed to go faster or slower, louder or softer, as needed.

If there is supposed to be a large crowd fighting offstage, the sound engineer can record a few people making the right noises. Then that can be re-recorded and layered over and over to make it seem like a large, noisy crowd.

The sound designer and the director decide how loud and long each sound effect should be. These sound cues are then programmed into a computer so that the sound operator can play them at appropriate moments during the show.

Music

Many of Shakespeare's plays have songs in them, to be accompanied by instruments such as strings, drums, woodwinds and lutes. Today, synthesizers are used as well as traditional instruments to produce a wide range of music. The music and arrangements for the songs Shakespeare wrote no longer exist, so composers have to invent new tunes that fit the style of the production.

Music helps, better than anything else, to set the scene. Composers try to create music that will put the audience in the right mood. *The Tempest* begins with a storm at sea; *As You Like It* starts on a summer's afternoon in an apple orchard. If you were a composer, what music and instruments might you use to set the right mood for these two very different scenes?

"Give me some more of that long low rumbling stuff," the director said over an intercom.

Booooooooom. With a push of a button, Owen made thunder roll around the great circular theatre.

Then suddenly strange echoey laughter blared from the speakers.

"What's that?" asked Rosie.

Owen glanced quickly over the control board and shook his head. "I don't know."

The laughter grew louder still.

"Maybe it's coming from down there," said Rosie, poking her head out the open window of the booth. As she did, her hand brushed the panel board.

Kaboom!

Owen shut off the sound, but it was too late. The director had spotted Rosie.

"No mice in the sound room!" he yelled.

Rosie turned to Owen. "It was an accident!" she pleaded.

Owen shrugged. "You heard the man."

"This is not fair! I didn't do anything!" said Rosie, stomping off. "Mouse! They all think I'm nothing but a pest!" She was so mad that she barked "Huh! Huh! Huh!" and listened to her voice bounce off the hallway walls. It was huge, magnificent, so unlike her normal voice. It made her think of the booming laugh in the theatre. Underneath that huge sound was something familiar. A laugh she thought she knew.

Just as she made one last giant "Huh" for good luck, someone laughed quietly beside her. "Ah, 'the sweet bird's throat.'"

"Don't you 'sweet bird' me!" said Rosie angrily. "You've got some explaining to do."

Shakespearean Language

Have you ever told anyone you could swim like a duck? Did you know you were quoting a line from *The Tempest*? Here are some words and expressions that were made famous in Shakespeare's plays.

When you describe a relative as "my own flesh and blood," or an offensive sight as "an eyesore," or a pleasing place as "heaven on earth," you are using words and ideas from Shakespeare. He didn't think up all these wonderful expressions in one fell swoop, mind you. But — you guessed it — he did think up the expression "one fell swoop"!

Poetry

Shakespeare wrote his plays in verse, not everyday speech. The words bounce along: there are five stressed beats in a line. Try saying Jaques's lines from *As You Like It*, putting the stress on the parts of the words printed in bold. (The speech begins partway through the first line, so it has only three stressed beats.)

All the **world's** a **stage**,
And **all** the **men** and **women merely players**:
They **have** their **exits and** their **entrances**,
And **one** man **in** his **time** plays **many parts** ...

Sometimes, however, when the character speaking is funny, or poor, or odd in some way, Shakespeare changed the rhythm. Try saying this famous witches' curse from *Macbeth*:

How many beats are in those lines? Did you notice that the lines start with a stressed beat? Does it feel different saying those lines than saying Jaques's?

Double, **D**ouble, **T**oil and **T**rouble,
Fire **burn** and **caul**dron **bub**ble.

Will chuckled.

"And stop laughing at me, you weed."

"Surely you can do better than that!" Will said, and he started to walk away. "How about 'moon calf' or 'testril' or 'cream-faced loon.'"

"You come back here, you ... you ... 'shag-eared villain!'" Rosie shouted.

"Much better!" said Will, and he disappeared into a room at the end of the hall. Rosie bounded in after him.

CHAPTER 6

*T*URN, *hell-hound, turn!*"

A soldier, with a sword raised above his head, came straight at Rosie. She ducked just as the soldier thrust his sword into another soldier's ribs. As she watched in horror, he gasped, groaned and fell dead to the floor beside her. It was Angelo!

A man clapped his hands, stepped over Angelo's body and grabbed the other soldier's arm. "No, no, no. You must keep the shoulder soft. Loose, yes?"

"Better stand over by the wall," Angelo's corpse whispered to Rosie. He smiled and jumped to his feet.

Safe in a corner, Rosie looked around the room, checking out each of the armoured, helmeted soldiers.

Where was Will? He had certainly run into this room — she had been right behind him.

The fight master clapped, and the ten actors quickly got back into position.

"En garde!"

All around Rosie there was a wild clashing of swords and stomping of feet. "Keep to your beats!" the fight master warned. The actors who were still learning their moves called out: "Thrust. Parry. Riposte. Parry. Reprise. Parry. Remise," as their swords crashed. One soldier jumped onto a tabletop as he fought. Suddenly he was gored through the stomach and did a magnificent fall through the air, howling as he died.

"No, this is not good." The fight instructor stopped the action again. "You must tuck the head more. No tension in the neck."

Rosie inched along the wall towards the door. It might be just pretend, but it was frightening.

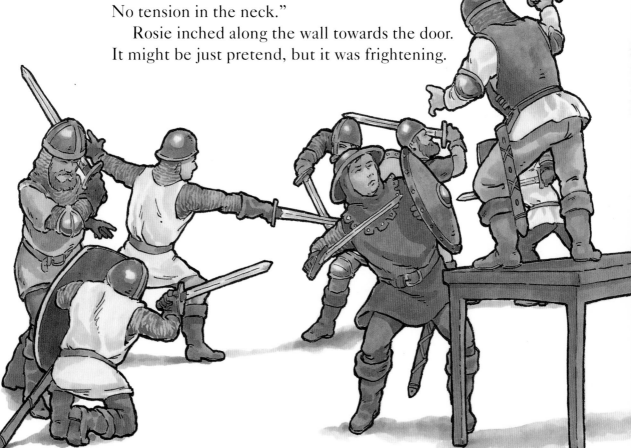

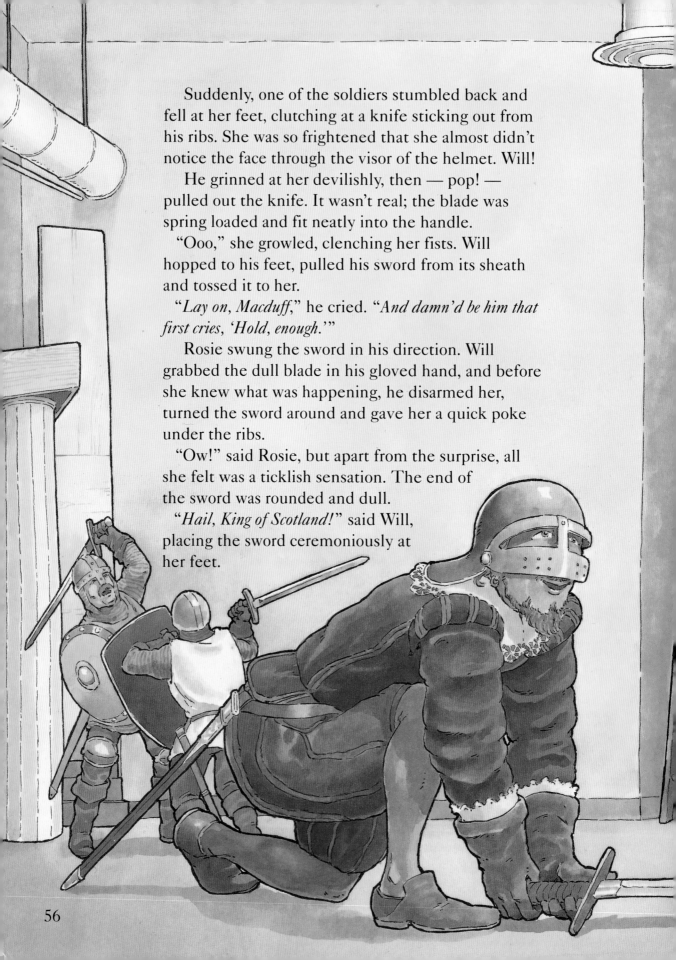

Suddenly, one of the soldiers stumbled back and fell at her feet, clutching at a knife sticking out from his ribs. She was so frightened that she almost didn't notice the face through the visor of the helmet. Will!

He grinned at her devilishly, then — pop! — pulled out the knife. It wasn't real; the blade was spring loaded and fit neatly into the handle.

"Ooo," she growled, clenching her fists. Will hopped to his feet, pulled his sword from its sheath and tossed it to her.

"*Lay on, Macduff*," he cried. "*And damn'd be him that first cries, 'Hold, enough.'*"

Rosie swung the sword in his direction. Will grabbed the dull blade in his gloved hand, and before she knew what was happening, he disarmed her, turned the sword around and gave her a quick poke under the ribs.

"Ow!" said Rosie, but apart from the surprise, all she felt was a ticklish sensation. The end of the sword was rounded and dull.

"*Hail, King of Scotland!*" said Will, placing the sword ceremoniously at her feet.

"You ... you ... moon calf!" yelled Rosie, as Will dashed from the room, and she took off in hot pursuit.

But Will was nowhere in sight. Rosie stopped to get her breath. As angry as she was at him, she realized that the fight had been the most fun she'd had in days. "Come back, you cream-faced loon!" she called, but there was no answer. The silence in the hall closed around her.

Suddenly she felt very lonely. She decided to go up to the box office. Maybe there would be a letter from her father. He had sent an envelope full of smelly eucalyptus leaves the last time and had promised a koala bear next. But there was no letter and no bear.

57

Administration, Box Office and Publicity

A theatre is divided into five areas: the stage area; backstage, where there are dressing rooms and the "green room" (a lounge area for the actors); the administrative offices; the "house," where the audience sits to see the play; and the "front of house," the lobby and box office areas.

Every theatre has people "behind the scenes" who make the organization run smoothly. An artistic director is everybody's boss, and makes all the big decisions, including which plays to do and who should direct them. A producer oversees how much money is spent and by which department. The publicists get people excited about coming to the theatre. They have posters and flyers printed, place ads in newspapers and magazines and arrange for radio, television and newspaper interviews with the cast and crew. People in the box office answer the phones, give out information about the shows and sell tickets. They also help actors and crew from out of town by finding lodgings for them and collecting their mail.

The house manager is in charge of the ushers and everything that goes on in the lobby area. He or she must make sure that the audience is sitting in their seats when the play is ready to begin.

In a small theatre, these jobs might be done by only a few people. In a large theatre, many people work in each department. In Shakespeare's day, the lead actors and writers looked after all the organizing, too. Where did they find the time!

BACKSTAGE

STAGE

ADMINISTRATIVE OFFICES

HOUSE

FRONT OF HOUSE

Rosie was just heading past the concession stand when a poster caught her eye. She stared at it. The pointy beard, the gold earring, the little smirk — it was Will. No doubt about it. But Shakespeare had been dead for hundreds of years.

"Aha," she said. "Some actor is playing a joke on me. Trying to get me in big trouble."

But who? And why?

"There were rumours you'd come this way." Cleo's voice snapped Rosie out of her reverie. "There's an army out looking for you."

"What?" said Rosie.

Her mother smiled, but her eyes looked worried. "I've been hearing some pretty crazy things about you."

"You ain't heard nothing yet," Rosie murmured, glancing at the poster again.

Cleo looked long and hard at Rosie. "I think you could use an outing."

Rosie gave her mother a half smile. This was definitely not the time to tell her about Will.

CHAPTER 7

CLEO had work to do at the theatre warehouse. Rosie was left to wander on her own. What a shock! Rosie had heard about this place, but she had no idea it would be so huge! There was aisle upon aisle of costumes, props and set pieces from hundreds of shows.

Kings' robes, peasants' rags, Roman togas and grand ladies' velvet capes nestled against one another on the clothing racks. There were shelves of guns: sleek pistols and trumpet-like blunderbusses. And there were swords: heavy broad ones and slim rapiers, pirates' cutlasses and wicked-looking snickersnees. There was armour of leather and armour of gold. Rosie found knick-knacks and garden tools and even what looked like a shelf of books but turned out to be only cut and painted mailing tubes. There were shelves of pies and fruits. There were animals: sheep and parrots and a great donkey's head hanging amid furry clothing on a rack. It had the sweetest brown eyes. Unable to resist, Rosie scratched the donkey's nose.

"Achooo!"

Rosie jumped back in shock. The donkey's mouth opened wide. "Boo!" said an all-too-familiar voice. Before Rosie could move, Will had pulled his head out of the donkey mask and dashed down the next aisle.

"Come back here, donkey-face!" yelled Rosie, taking off after him. Up and down the aisles she ran, seeing glimpses of Will but never catching up. Then she turned the last corner, and there he was, trapped by a display of market vegetables.

"That director hates me," said Rosie, closing in on him. "And it's all your fault!"

"Ah well, you'll get used to directors," said Will. Then he turned and leap-frogged over a barrel of potatoes. Rosie clambered after him, along the dark, high-walled corridor. As she ran, she saw light ahead and heard noises: people and street sounds. There were smells, too: sharp animal smells and roasted food and the smell of dust in the sun. Suddenly she broke out of the enclosed alley into an old-fashioned town square.

"Get yer 'ot meat pies!" cried a boy carrying a tray on his head.

"Apricocks!" shouted another hawker.

"Caraway seeds!"

"Stories for a penny!"

"Comfits! Suckets!"

Under a bright noon-time sun, crowds of people bustled about. Rosie could barely understand them, though they seemed to be speaking English. And their clothes! Could she have stumbled into the middle of a play? Outside?

Folks were staring at her.

Rosie tried to step back but couldn't. The hodgepodge of people formed a ragtag line outside a large round building. Although it looked very old-fashioned, the wood and plaster were clean and new looking.

"'Ope you've got a penny fer the hentertainment, luv." A fat lady with a squawling baby under one arm eyed Rosie suspiciously.

The coin the lady showed her was bigger than any penny Rosie had ever seen. She didn't even recognize the queen on it.

"Rosalind. Where have you been?"

Will took her by the hand and led her out of the line towards the arched doorway of the building.

"Where have *I* been?!" she said, shaking free of his grasp. "Where —"

"Oh, stop yer pribble friggling," he said, marching past the line-up and through the doorway.

"Where are we?" she asked. "Don't we have to pay?"

"The Globe Theatre," said Will proudly. "It's opening day. And it's perfectly all right, my juggy — you're my guest. Sprightly, now."

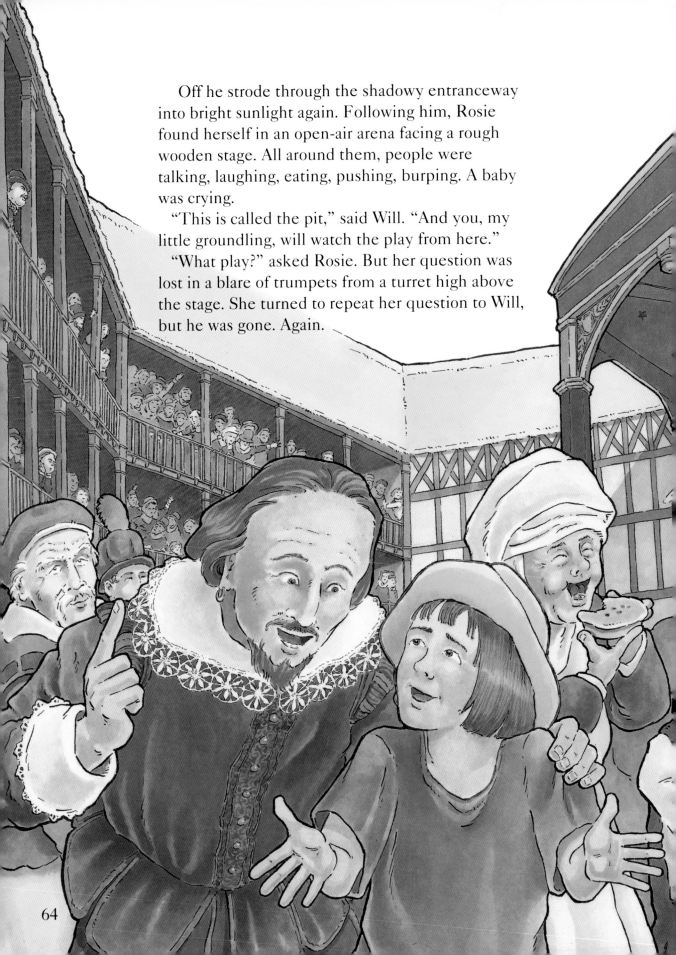

Off he strode through the shadowy entranceway into bright sunlight again. Following him, Rosie found herself in an open-air arena facing a rough wooden stage. All around them, people were talking, laughing, eating, pushing, burping. A baby was crying.

"This is called the pit," said Will. "And you, my little groundling, will watch the play from here."

"What play?" asked Rosie. But her question was lost in a blare of trumpets from a turret high above the stage. She turned to repeat her question to Will, but he was gone. Again.

The Wooden O

The Globe theatre was a circular wooden building built in 1599.

Above the door was a picture of Hercules holding the world on his shoulders and the words *Totus mundus agit historionem*. That's Latin for "All the world's a stage," which is a line from *As You Like It*, the first play ever performed there.

The stage was a platform, surrounded on three sides by a flat area of bare earth known as the "pit" where spectators called "groundlings" watched the play. They also talked, ate, drank and walked around, even while the play was on! They were sometimes called "penny skinkards" because they paid a penny to get in and were usually noisy, raucous and probably smelly.

The pit where the groundlings stood was open to the sky, but the stage area was covered by a roof called the "shadow" or "heavens." The underside of this roof was painted with stars or signs of the zodiac, and the posts that supported it could be used in the play as trees or pillars. There were doors on either side of the stage and a trapdoor on the stage itself, which could be used for quick or mysterious entrances and exits and perhaps as a cave for monsters.

The audience area was modelled on the courtyard of a typical village inn, which is where acting companies performed in the countryside. The wall around the open pit held three levels that looked down on the stage. It cost two pennies to get into these stands, but you got a seat and you got a roof. There was a

thatched straw roof to protect the "gods," the highest level of stands, from the weather.

Behind the stage was a "tiring house." It was the dressing room for the actors and got its name from the word "attire." On the second level of the tiring house was a

playing area for scenes that had to be performed above the main action. There were also windows in the tiring house to play scenes from.

The next storey in the tiring house held musicians and sound-effects makers. The building was crowned with a turret, from which trumpeters blew their horns to proclaim the start of the play.

There was no electric or gas lighting in Shakespeare's day, so plays were performed in the middle of the afternoon. The theatre could hold two to three thousand people and was busy every day except Sunday, when it was closed.

On June 29, 1613, the play *Henry VIII* was being performed at the Globe Theatre. In act 1, scene 4, a cannon was fired as usual to signal the arrival of King Henry. No one noticed sparks settle in the thatched roof. The straw smouldered for a few minutes, then burst into flames. In just one hour, the entire Globe Theatre had burned to the ground. No one was hurt, but one gentleman in the audience discovered his pants were on fire. The quick-thinking fellow put them out with a handy bottle of beer!

The Globe Theatre was rebuilt right away and reopened within a year.

"Wot d'you say, puggy?" A toothless old fellow smiled at Rosie.

"What play are they doing?"

"Oh, well, it's a new un by that Shakesper. 'E calls it *As You Like It*, and I 'ope we do or I'll throw these tomates at 'im an' start a brabble!" He gestured to a basket of rotting fruit beside him and roared with happy anticipation.

As You Like It? Rosie knew all about that play because Rosalind, the character she was named after, was in it. She also knew that it was first performed in 1599! Rosie looked around carefully. People jostled for position, crowding tightly in spite of the heat. Scruffy children played tag, and there was a lot of good-natured shoving. People snacked and drank beer. There was even a fist fight. Wherever this was — whenever it was — it certainly wasn't anywhere she had seen before.

Rosie's attention was drawn to the stage. The language that seemed so strange to her was obviously not strange to this holiday crowd. They nodded and laughed and poked one another in the ribs at jokes Rosie did not understand. Then there *she* was on stage — well, her namesake, anyway, Rosalind. But this Rosalind was not pretty like Alice. Hey! She wasn't even a girl!

Boy Actors

Women and girls were not allowed to be actors in Shakespeare's day. Older male comedians played the parts of older women. Usually these roles were comic parts, and it was funnier if the "women" looked rather large and hairy. The girls' parts were played by boys, apprentices training to take on male roles when they got older. Boy actors were not full-grown, had high voices and didn't shave yet, so they could, with a little work, impersonate women. Certain boys became quite famous for their ability to portray beautiful young girls.

In many of Shakespeare's plays, girl characters dress up as boys to go somewhere in disguise, so they were actually boy actors dressed up as girls dressed up as boys! In *As You Like It*, it's even more complicated. The boy actor playing the girl, Rosalind, dresses as a boy named Ganymede, who then pretends to be the girl, Rosalind!

Rosie found it a little hard to concentrate on the play. There were so many distractions around her. But one actor captured her attention. The part of Jaques was a small one, but there was something special about the actor.

"It's Will!" she burst out suddenly.

"Ah, yes, duck, that there's Mr. Shakesper," said the toothless man. "'E's a right hodgepoker, 'e is, but 'e's doin' a delitable job." He seemed almost disappointed. "I guess I won't be givin' 'im a tizzy-muzzy of tomates, after all." He nattered on so that Rosie had to strain to hear what Will was saying.

"All the world's a stage,
And all the men and women merely players,
They have their exits and their entrances,
And one man in his time plays many parts ..."

The sun was beating down. The crowd pressed in. Rosie was enchanted by the performance, but how hot it was! Oh, for a penny so she could sit in the gods. The noise, the jostling. It was hard to concentrate ... the play ... she felt so dizzy ... the sun ...

"Rosie!"

Someone was calling her from far away.

"Will? Is that you?"

"Wake up, Rosie. Are you all right?"

Rosie looked around. No Globe. No groundlings. No *As You Like It*. Just Rosie on a pile of Styrofoam potatoes, and Cleo, looking worried.

"I'm not surprised you fell asleep — this warehouse is so hot and stuffy. Let's get some fresh air." Her mother shook her head. "And maybe a shower. How did you get so filthy?"

Rosie looked at herself. She was covered from head to toe in dust and soot.

CHAPTER 8

ROSIE sat at the stage door looking out at the night and a summer storm as noisy as anything Owen could cook up in the sound room! Everyone was working late — and in a bad mood.

Things were going very wrong. Now the kid who was supposed to play Macduff's son had broken his leg. He'd be in a cast for weeks — but not in the cast of *Macbeth*. But the big news was worse. The famous old actor who played Prospero had not come to rehearsal — and no one knew why.

"Still mad at me?"

There was Will, with such a sweet, silly expression on his face that any anger she felt dissolved.

"No more hide and seek!" she said. "Want to go

splash in the puddles instead?"

Will looked pleased but shook his head and squatted beside her, looking out at the rainy night.

"I can't," he said. "Besides, I've got homework." He opened a big black scrapbook on his lap. On one page was taped a copy of a page of text from a play; on the opposite page there were little pictures and notes, lines and arrows. As she watched, Will put a line through a couple of lines of text and then paused, tapping his pencil on the page.

Rosie read some of the lines. "Hey!" she said. "That's Margaret's prompt book for *Mac* — the Scottish play!"

"It may be Margaret's prompt book," said Will, "but it's *my* play."

Rosie's head was swimming — Margaret was frantic about that book. "You can't just change it like that!"

"You're right, I can't," said Will, "but I wish I could. I've always hated those lines. But I just can't seem to come up with anything better."

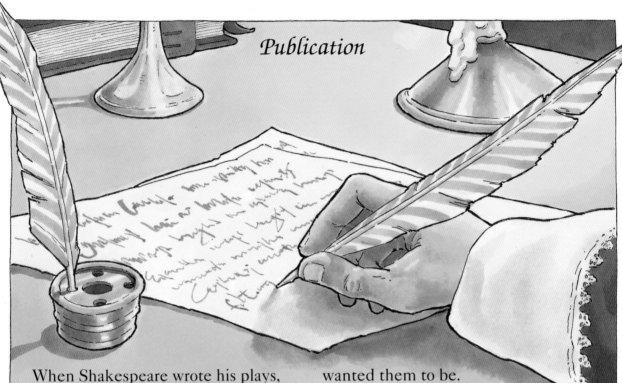

When Shakespeare wrote his plays, he didn't imagine people would be reading and performing them hundreds of years after his death. He tried to perfect each show as it was done but didn't pay much attention to the script when the production was over.

Only half of his plays were printed during his lifetime. Shakespeare didn't check the type carefully, and they ended up being printed with lots of mistakes. After Shakespeare died, another playwright, Ben Jonson, thought the plays were so important that they should be printed carefully. He gathered the plays using bits of Shakespeare's handwritten manuscripts, notes from stage productions and whatever lines and directions anyone could remember. But no one can be sure if they are the way Shakespeare would have wanted them to be.

In the centuries since Shakespeare's death, people have changed the plays to suit themselves: speeches have been cut or added; stories have been rearranged; and tragedies have been given happy endings. Several plays have even been turned into musicals! They've been translated into hundreds of languages, and made into movies — something Shakespeare couldn't have imagined.

Today people study Shakespeare by closely comparing handwritten manuscripts of the plays (when they can find them) with printed texts. Scholars try to sort out the changes Shakespeare made from those made by someone else. People will probably always tinker with Shakespeare's plays to come up with a new, better, "just right" version.

"A writer never really stops writing a play," Will said. "Some lines sound just right no matter how many times you hear them and others ... well ..."

"It's like my dad," said Rosie. "He's always tinkering with his guitar. Always trying to find new sounds or a smoother way to play."

"That's it," said Will. "I must tinker — such a lovely word — with my words. I make them smoother or angrier or more lovely — make them new."

Lightning flashed. Rosie counted ten steamboats before the thunder rumbled. The storm was moving away.

"You really are William Shakespeare, aren't you?"

"At your service, my dear Rosalind."

It was impossible, and yet here he was. "What are you doing here?" she asked.

"Working, of course," said Will. "There are so many things to deal with, from these words to the jewels on a lordly cape."

"You —"

"Oh, shush, child," said Will. "The oval stones look much better than those horrid fat diamonds. Besides, I have a right. Without me, none of this would be happening."

William Shakespeare

William Shakespeare was born in the town of Stratford-Upon-Avon, England, in April 1564. It was a pretty town of about two hundred houses, surrounded by forests and open meadows. Will's father made gloves and other leather goods, and his mother was the daughter of a wealthy farmer.

Will began attending the Stratford Grammar School when he was seven years old. School went from six or seven in the morning until eleven, and then from one in the afternoon until five or six — six days a week! Most of the stories and themes in Will's plays came from the Latin, Greek and Bible he studied at school.

Will married Anne Hathaway when he was 18 years old. When he was 21, he left Stratford, Anne and their three children to seek his fortune in London. Although he continued to support his family in Stratford, he lived in London for most of his life.

London was then a busy, noisy city of five hundred thousand people. Plays were a very popular form of entertainment, and there were three theatres in London when William arrived: The Theatre, The Curtain and The Rose. William got a job as a "hired man" with a theatre company. He had small acting roles, worked backstage and helped with the writing. It was hard work because the

The Globe

theatre companies sometimes did as many as 15 different plays in one month! Will's first play, *Henry VI, Part I*, was performed on March 3, 1592. He eventually became part owner of a theatre company called the Lord Chamberlain's Men, which performed all his plays.

Shakespeare is thought to have written 38 plays in 24 years. They are

usually grouped as Histories, about real characters (mostly kings) and historic events; Comedies; Tragedies; and Romances. A couple of his plays were co-written with someone else, and he may have written others that are now lost. He also wrote 154 love sonnets (14-line poems) and at least three epic poems — long stories told in verse.

Some people think Shakespeare didn't really write his plays, because he wasn't that well educated. But more amazing is that *anyone* could have written them. How could one person be so clever and inspired to write so many plays in such a short time — plays that still make audiences all over the world laugh and cry four hundred years after they were written?

Rosie thought of all the hard-working theatre people — Stratford was theirs, too. But what Will had said was true: the whole theatre celebrated his life.

"Am I the only one who knows you're here?" she asked.

"That's hard to say."

"Nobody else seems to see you. And nearly every time I do, I end up in trouble!"

"I'm a difficult person to know," said Will.

"I'll say."

"I'm always prowling around when someone puts on one of my plays," said Will, "but hardly anyone notices. They're all too busy."

He suddenly looked sad.

"What's the matter?" Rosie asked.

Will sighed. "Prospero is not well. That old magician may not be my greatest character, but he's my favourite."

"Why?"

Will smiled. "*The Tempest* was the last play I wrote all on my own. It's about magic — the magic of the stage, magic that can take you away to a faraway island in a magic sea. And Prospero is me." He chuckled. "Or I'm Prospero."

Rosie remembered how the famous actor's face had shone as she had looked up from the trapdoor. He had made her feel that everything would turn out okay.

"He'll be all right," she said.

"Oh, he's a trooper for sure," said Will, seeming a bit happier.

Footsteps were approaching the stage door. Rosie and Will could hear the director talking to the stage-door guard. She grabbed his hand and they hid behind a trolley of fake shrubbery.

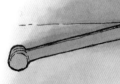

The director stared out the door before heading for his car. Rosie thought he looked very tired and thoughtful, not like a grouch. They watched him head out into the rain.

"I've been following that man's career for some time," said Will.

"I've just been trying to stay out of his way."

"He usually isn't so bad," said Will. "But he's under a lot of pressure. He's in charge of the whole show. If it doesn't work, it's his fault."

The Director

The director of a play is like an orchestra conductor. His or her first job is to read the play through many times to find what is special or interesting about it. The director must make the point of the play clear and the relationships between the characters easy to understand. Each director will see a play differently. Each will find different things in the words and actions that are important.

The director usually decides which actors should play which parts. Then the director and the designers decide what period, style and mood the play will be in. All the words, actors, costumes, props, sets, make-up, light and sound must work together so that the world they create on stage makes sense.

Rosie and Will watched the director's car turn out of the parking lot. Behind them in the theatre, sewing machines whirred and hammers tapped tiny nails into the heels of large boots.

Rosie thought again of Margaret, searching for the prompt book. "Are you finished with this?" she asked quietly.

Will sighed. "I guess so. It's not perfect, but it will have to do until I can think of something better." He handed the book to Rosie.

They stared out at the rain together.

I'll give the book back to Margaret first thing in the morning, Rosie thought. Just as soon as I can come up with a good explanation of how I found it!

CHAPTER 9

*R*OSIE opened her bedroom window and took a deep breath. The sun was shining again, but it was going to be a difficult morning. Rosie took the prompt book from under her pillow. Will hadn't done any real damage to the book — his pencil lines were easily erased. But the way things were going, she was bound to wind up in trouble over this. Maybe if I just leave it somewhere, Margaret can find it herself, she thought. But no, that was what criminals did in mystery books, and they always got caught.

"Rosie, are you dressed yet?" Cleo called as she raced into the kitchen. "Hurry up — I'm in a real rush today!"

Rosie hid the prompt book in her backpack and

worked on her story as her mother bustled about.

As soon as they arrived at the theatre, Rosie took the prompt book from her backpack and ran off to find Margaret.

"I was just in the green room," said Rosie, "and there was a big pile of magazines —"

"Rosie, you're a marvel!" Margaret interrupted her, scooping up the book and giving her a big hug. "Maybe now our luck will change."

Rosie could hardly believe her ears.

Down in props, Cleo was fidgeting with Prospero's magic staff. It would light up when he "drew" with it in the air or on the ground.

"I'd really like to show him how we've got this rigged up," said Cleo. "But no one knows when — or if — he's coming in. The director is fuming."

"I could take it over to him," Rosie suddenly suggested, surprised at hearing herself make the offer. "He and I get along really well."

"Great idea!" said Jamie. "It's just down the block. Rosie could probably use a break from this place, don't you think?"

Cleo didn't look convinced.

"And this place could use a break from me," said Rosie.

Jamie laughed. Cleo smiled and handed her the staff. "Just don't pester him, okay?"

❖ ❖ ❖

The actor lived in a big old house with a magnificent garden overlooking the river. As Rosie walked up the path to the front door, she felt foolish and afraid. She had a little speech about Will and how much Prospero meant to him; but it suddenly seemed crazy. Who would ever believe it? She took a deep breath and knocked on the door with the magic staff.

She waited. She knocked again. The staff lit up with every knock. Still no answer. He *had* to be there. The sun was hot now. Maybe he was in his back garden.

The light in the garden dazzled her, reflecting off millions of dewdrops on the petals of a thousand flowers. On the patio sat Prospero, wrapped in a blanket and sipping a cup of tea.

"Hi," she called out. The actor turned with a frown. "It's me, Rosie ... from the theatre? I've brought you your magic staff."

The actor's frown dissolved. "Caliban's underling," he said, laughing, "with Prospero's magic wand. My, my — what a dangerous state of affairs!"

Rosie made her way through the garden gate. The air was heavy with the scent of roses. She tapped the staff on the patio stone to show him how it worked. She handed it to him. As he held it, his expression became serene. He put aside his blanket and stood

up. He tapped the staff, twirled it and played with it until his face shone with pleasure. The prop seemed to come alive. It *was* magic.

"A friend of mine says you're a real trooper," she blurted out.

"How kind," said the actor, writing in the air with his staff.

"An actor friend," said Rosie. "He once played Prospero himself, years ago. It's his favourite part."

The actor stopped and raised a craggy eyebrow. "An *old* friend?" he asked.

"Very old," Rosie replied. And then she winked. "Very, very old."

The actor rested on his staff. He stared at her for a long moment.

"And is this friend a writer, too, perchance?"

Rosie nodded. "A very busy one."

He cleared his throat. "When I was a very young actor," he said, "I met a strange fellow. Loved the theatre. Had theatre, not blood, in his veins, I kidded him. It took me a while to realize I was the only one in the theatre who had ever met this particular fellow. When I mentioned him, the other actors thought I was crackers."

"So you know him, too!"

The old actor gazed at her a moment. "Yes," he said. "He's the one who persuaded me to stay in the theatre."

"He still needs you," said Rosie quietly.

The old actor suddenly looked very frail, and Rosie was afraid that she had said the wrong thing. But the cloud on his face passed.

"You're a special and lucky girl." He grinned at her. "Now you must excuse me. I have much work to do."

He waved a farewell with the staff as Rosie closed the gate behind her.

At the theatre, Rosie was greeted by another hug from Margaret. "Our Prospero just phoned and said he'll be here for rehearsal this afternoon. I don't know what you did, but he says you cured him."

To Rosie's surprise, everyone congratulated her. In a theatre, word gets around fast!

"Now you seem to be bringing us good luck!" said Des, showing her the finished costume for Macduff's son. It didn't look dull at all!

Rosie was aching to tell Will the good news, but he wasn't to be found. As the day progressed, she became more and more disappointed, just as everyone else became more and more excited. The first play of the season, *As You Like It*, was to preview that night — its first performance in front of an audience. Everyone was jittery and bubbly.

Backstage, dukes and nobles mingled with peasants and shepherds. Rosie could hardly recognize anyone in their make-up and wigs. Was that Angelo, the monster Caliban, looking so elegant in velvet and silk? Could that be Stephen dressed as a clown?

Actors are always having to look like people they are not. They make changes in their voices, movements and clothing for each different character they play. But a good make-up job can sometimes create the biggest change.

Make-up is very important because it helps an audience to see an actor's face from a distance. It uses contrasts of light and dark to highlight the actor's expressions. Make-up was originally made from clay, charcoal and vegetable dyes mixed with oil or animal fat. Sometimes ham rind was smeared on the face and then powdered charcoal or clay dust patted on. (This is where we get the expression "a ham," meaning someone who overacts or tries too hard to get attention.)

Today, special water- or cream-based make-ups are used to change skin tone and texture. Eyes, eyebrows, noses and mouths can appear to change size and shape. Flesh-coloured modelling clay can be used to build up a nose, forehead or cheekbones. An actor can have a long crooked nose, dark deep-set eyes and a wide red clownish mouth one night, and then appear beautiful with bright eyes and pink "rosebud" lips the next night.

Sometimes actors need more, or less, hair. Crepe hair is stuck on with special glue called spirit gum to make a moustache or beard. Wigmakers work to create the right hairstyles and colours for the many characters on stage. A bald head can be made by sticking down the actor's hair with soap or gel, then covering the head with a plastic or nylon cap. Make-up can then be applied right on top of the cap. With the right make-up job, an actor can be bald one night and have long, flowing curls the next.

And there was Alice in her court dress. What a beautiful Rosalind she was, thought Rosie, remembering the boy actor at The Globe. She gave Alice a big but careful hug so as not to muss her costume. "Break a leg!" she said.

Although Rosie was a little afraid of running into the director, she couldn't resist taking one last look at the set before the crowd was let in. Approaching the stage, she thought she heard a voice coming from the theatre.

Silently she peeked out. The orchard was in place for the first scene of *As You Like It*, but there was Will, at centre stage, speaking Prospero's final words from *The Tempest*.

"Now my charms are all o'erthrown,
And what strength I have's mine own,
Which is most faint."

His voice was strong, but somehow empty, lonely. She listened closely.

"But release me from my bands
With the help of your good hands.
Gentle breath of yours my sails
Must fill, or else my project fails,
Which was to please."

Rosie thought about those lines, about Will wanting his plays to please people. She thought about all the people at the theatre working to bring his words to life. She suddenly wanted to be able to thank him, although she wasn't quite sure for what.

"As you from crimes would pardon'd be,
Let your indulgence set me free."

As Will finished his bows to the empty, dark and waiting house, Rosie put her "good hands" together, clapping wildly. That's what he meant — applause would release him from the spell of the play.

She stepped out on the stage to join him. Gleefully, she told him about her visit with the old actor, and how he had met Will long ago.

"I can spot them a mile away," said Will proudly. "The special ones."

"That's what he called me," said Rosie. "He says I'm special."

"Hah! You? You're nothing but a mouse!"

Rosie could hardly believe her ears. "How can you say that?" she cried.

But Will only winked mischievously and turned to leave the stage. "Why, you're just a child," he taunted her. "You, an actor? Ridiculous." Rosie's shock turned quickly to anger as Will disappeared into the deep shadows of the tunnel exit, chuckling.

"You old pribble friggler!" she yelled. "Why would I ever want to be an actor? Huh! Huh! Huh! Take that — thou shag-ear'd villain."

She was outraged! As she listened to his laughter die away, she thought of the first time she had heard him laugh, when she and Caliban had popped their heads out on stage and the director had been so mad at her. The beating of her heart seemed to fill the theatre. Then she realized someone was clapping in the dark. From out of the shadows came a voice.

"So the Mouse acts, does it?"

The director.

Rosie's legs felt like jelly.

"Your little performance was very convincing." And as he came up onto the stage, she saw that he was actually smiling. It was quite a nice smile, for a grouch.

"You've got the part," he said.

"The part?"

"Macduff's son in the Scottish play. It will be weeks before that actor gets better. And it'll be a nice change — a girl playing a boy's part, instead of the other way around, the way it was in Shakespeare's day."

Rosie felt the whole world tremble and spin.

"Oh, come on now. You can do it," said the director, clapping her fondly on the shoulder. "It's not a very big part. And it seems you know quite a lot about Shakespeare."

"What are you two cooking up?" a voice behind her asked. Rosie turned to see Cleo smiling broadly.